# NATIONAL FOOTBALL LEAGUE

BY DAVID RAUSCH

BELLWETHER MEDIA • MINNEAPOLIS, MN

EPIC BOOKS are no ordinary books. They burst with intense action, high-speed heroics, and shadows of the unknown. Are you ready for an Epic adventure?

This edition first published in 2015 by Bellwether Media, Inc.

No part of this publication may be reproduced in whole or in part without written permission of the publisher. For information regarding permission, write to Bellwether Media, Inc., Attention: Permissions Department, 5357 Penn Avenue South, Minneapolis, MN 55419.

Library of Congress Cataloging-in-Publication Data

Rausch, David.
  National Football League / by David Rausch.
    pages cm. – (Epic : Major League Sports)
  Includes bibliographical references and index.
  Summary: "Engaging images accompany information about the National Football League. The combination of high-interest subject matter and light text is intended for students in grades 2 through 7"– Provided by publisher.
  ISBN 978-1-62617-136-7 (hardcover : alk. paper)
  1.  National Football League–History–Juvenile literature. 2.  Football–United States–History–Juvenile literature.  I. Title.
  GV955.5.N35R39 2014
  796.332′64–dc23
                          2014008472

Printed in the United States of America, North Mankato, MN.

# TABLE OF CONTENTS

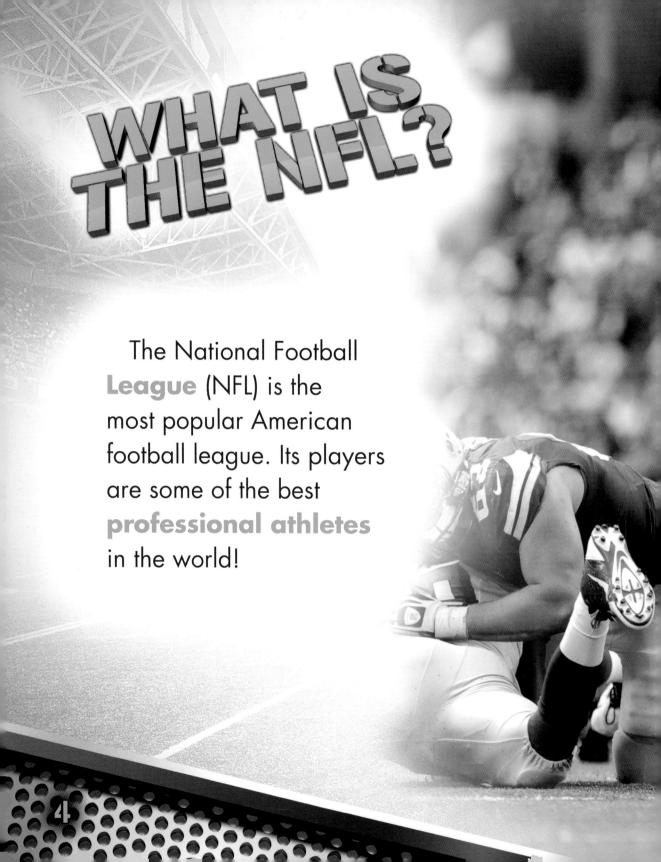

# WHAT IS THE NFL?

The National Football **League** (NFL) is the most popular American football league. Its players are some of the best **professional athletes** in the world!

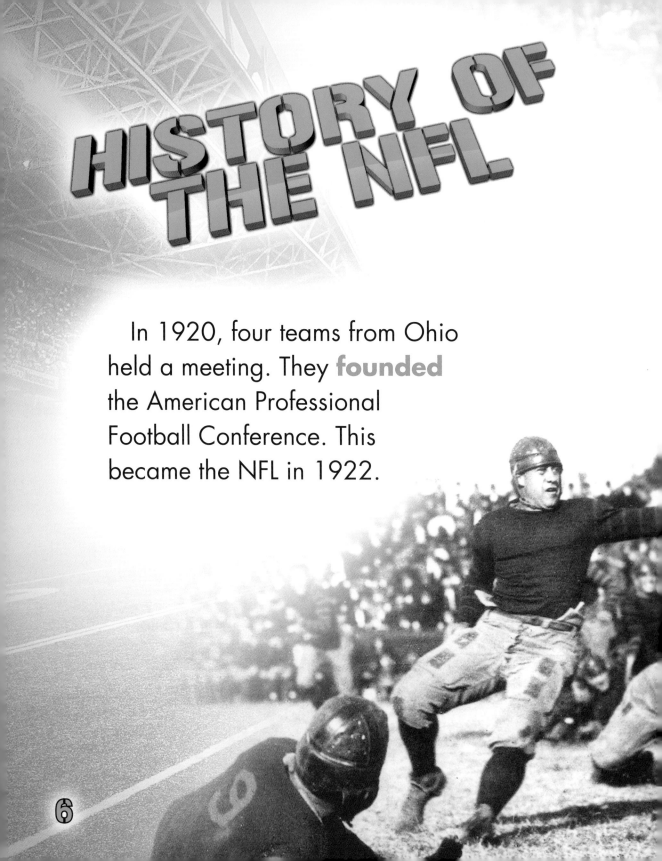

# HISTORY OF THE NFL

In 1920, four teams from Ohio held a meeting. They **founded** the American Professional Football Conference. This became the NFL in 1922.

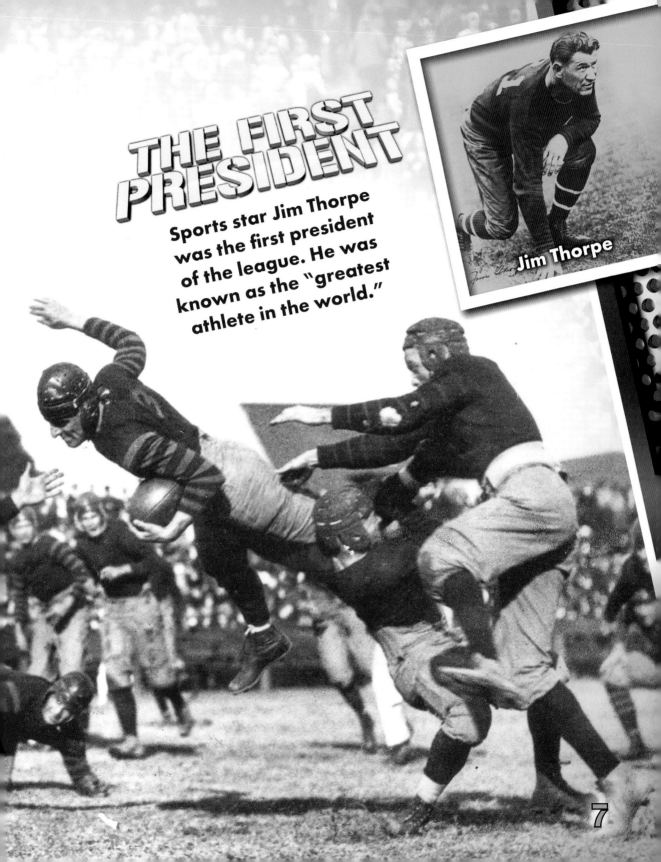

# THE FIRST PRESIDENT

Sports star Jim Thorpe was the first president of the league. He was known as the "greatest athlete in the world."

Jim Thorpe

7

Another league formed in 1959. It was called the American Football League (AFL). The AFL and NFL joined together in 1970.

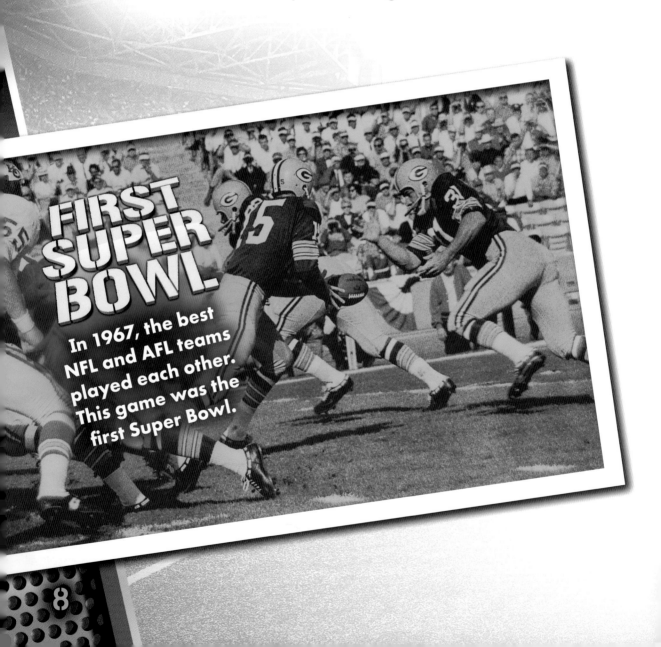

FIRST SUPER BOWL

In 1967, the best NFL and AFL teams played each other. This game was the first Super Bowl.

# A LOOK BACK

**August 20, 1920:** Four football teams from Ohio form a league. They call it the American Professional Football Conference.

**September 17, 1920:** More teams join the league. The name changes to the American Professional Football Association.

**June 24, 1922:** The name changes again. It is now called the National Football League.

**1934:** The NFL changes the shape of its football. The ball becomes longer and skinnier.

**February 8, 1936:** Teams pick college players in the first NFL draft. Jay Berwanger is the first player ever drafted.

Jay Berwanger

**October 22, 1939:** An NFL game is on television for the first time.

**August 14, 1959:** The American Football League is created. This league joins the NFL in 1970.

**September 7, 1963:** The Pro Football Hall of Fame opens in Canton, Ohio.

**January 15, 1967:** The Green Bay Packers beat the Kansas City Chiefs in the first Super Bowl.

Pro Football Hall of Fame

# THE TEAMS

Today, the NFL has 32 teams. They are separated into the American Football Conference (AFC) and National Football **Conference** (NFC). Both conferences have four **divisions** of 4 teams.

# AFC

## AFC East
- Buffalo Bills
- Miami Dolphins
- New England Patriots
- New York Jets

## AFC North
- Baltimore Ravens
- Cincinnati Bengals
- Cleveland Browns
- Pittsburgh Steelers

## AFC South
- Houston Texans
- Indianapolis Colts
- Jacksonville Jaguars
- Tennessee Titans

## AFC West
- Denver Broncos
- Kansas City Chiefs
- Oakland Raiders
- San Diego Chargers

# NFC

## NFC East
- Dallas Cowboys
- New York Giants
- Philadelphia Eagles
- Washington Redskins

## NFC North
- Chicago Bears
- Detroit Lions
- Green Bay Packers
- Minnesota Vikings

## NFC South
- Atlanta Falcons
- Carolina Panthers
- New Orleans Saints
- Tampa Bay Buccaneers

## NFC West
- Arizona Cardinals
- St. Louis Rams
- San Francisco 49ers
- Seattle Seahawks

NFL draft

Each team has 53 players. They play offense, defense, or **special teams**. Teams pick **rookies** from the **NFL draft**. They also trade players and add **free agents**.

# PLAYING THE GAME

Every NFL game starts with a coin toss. Then four 15-minute **quarters** follow. Both teams try to score touchdowns and field goals. **Officials** throw flags when rules are broken.

official

flag

## TIE GAME

A tie game goes into overtime. This lasts for 15 minutes. The extra period can end with a tie.

# FOOTBALL TALK

**extra point**—when the offense kicks the football through the goal posts after a touchdown; 1 point

**field goal**—when the offense kicks the football through the goal posts; 3 points

**first down**—when the offense gains 10 yards; results in four more plays.

**fumble**—when a player loses hold of the football

**interception**—when the defense catches a pass thrown by the offense

**safety**—when the offense is tackled in their own end zone; defense scores 2 points

**touchdown**—when a player carries or catches the football in their opponent's end zone; 6 points

**two-point conversion**—when the offense carries or catches the football in their opponent's end zone after scoring a touchdown; 2 points

# THE REGULAR SEASON

NFL players go to training camp in July. Next they play 4 preseason games. Then the regular season begins. Each team plays 16 games and has one **bye week**.

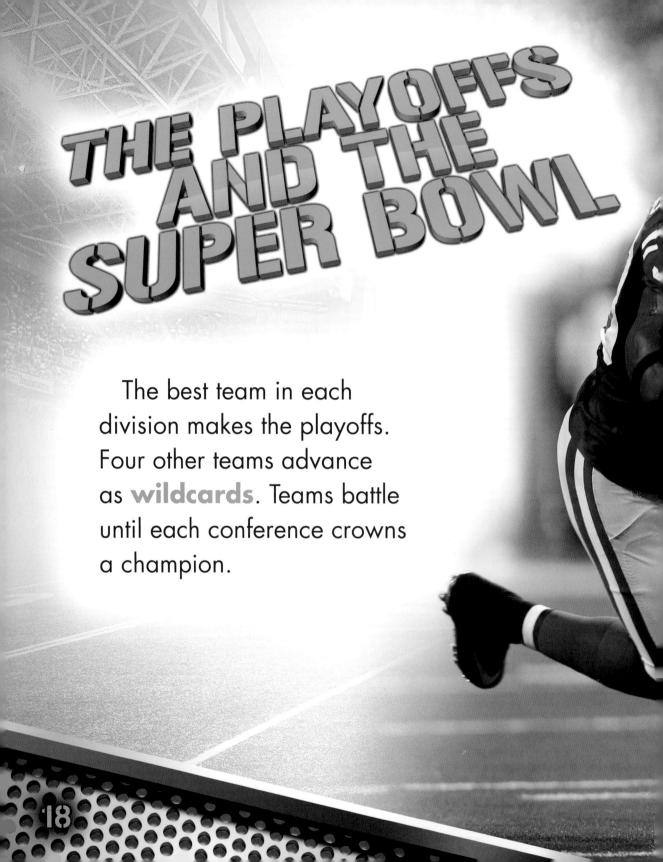

# THE PLAYOFFS AND THE SUPER BOWL

The best team in each division makes the playoffs. Four other teams advance as **wildcards**. Teams battle until each conference crowns a champion.

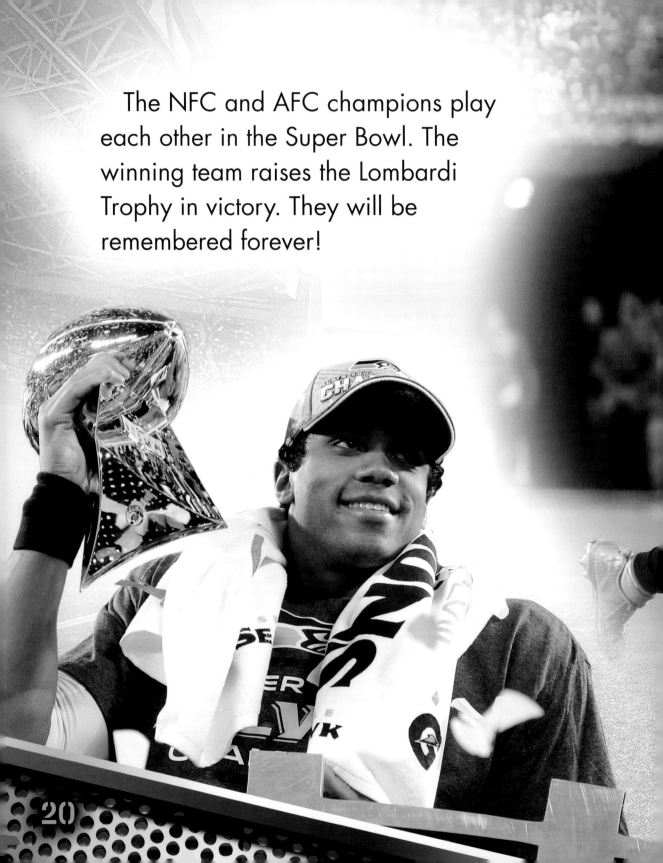

The NFC and AFC champions play each other in the Super Bowl. The winning team raises the Lombardi Trophy in victory. They will be remembered forever!

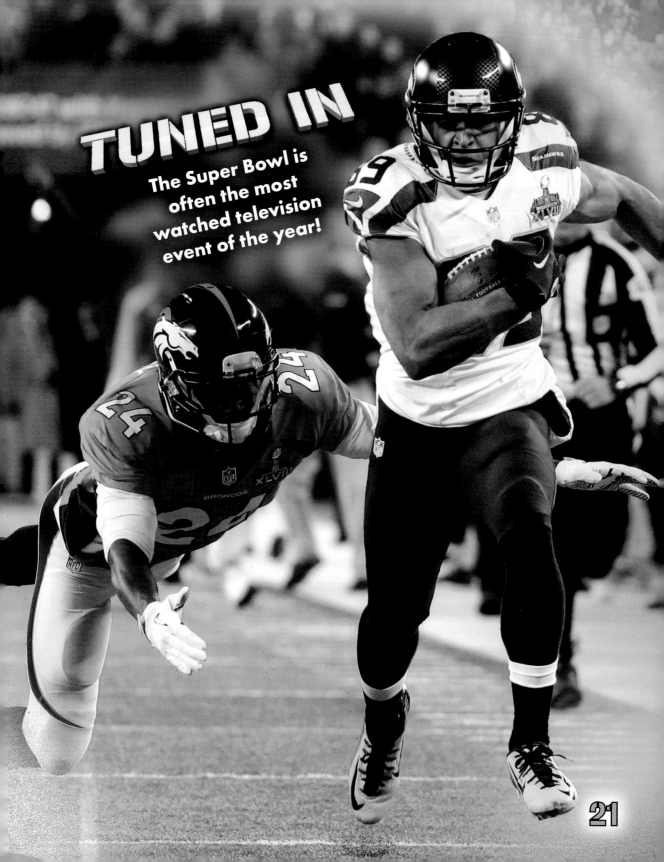

# TUNED IN

The Super Bowl is often the most watched television event of the year!

# GLOSSARY

**bye week**—a week in which a sports team does not play

**conference**—a group of sports teams within a league; teams in a conference often play one another.

**divisions**—groups of sports teams within a conference; teams in a division often play one another.

**founded**—created or formed

**free agents**—professional athletes who are free to play for any team; free agents do not have contracts.

**league**—a group of people or teams united by a common interest or activity

**NFL draft**—a yearly event in which NFL teams pick college players to play for them

**officials**—people who enforce the rules during a game

**professional athletes**—athletes who get paid to play a sport

**quarters**—the four periods of time in a football or basketball game

**rookies**—professional athletes in their first year

**special teams**—a group of players used during kickoffs, punts, and other special plays

**wildcards**—teams that make the playoffs without winning the division

# TO LEARN MORE

## At the Library

Doeden, Matt. *Play Football Like a Pro: Key Skills and Tips.* Mankato, Minn.: Capstone Press, 2011.

Latimer, Clay. *VIP Pass to a Pro Football Game Day.* Mankato, Minn.: Capstone Press, 2011.

Thomas, Keltie. *How Football Works.* Berkeley, Calif.: Owlkids, 2010.

## On the Web

Learning more about the National Football League is as easy as 1, 2, 3.

1. Go to www.factsurfer.com.

2. Enter "National Football League" into the search box.

3. Click the "Surf" button and you will see a list of related web sites.

With factsurfer.com, finding more information is just a click away.

# INDEX

The images in this book are reproduced through the courtesy of: Brian Peterson/ Abaca USA/ Newscom, front cover (left); Associated Press, front cover (right), pp. 6-7, 14, 21; Albert Pena/ Cal Sport Media/ ZUMA Press/ Newscom, pp. 4-5, 10; Bettmann/ Corbis, pp. 7 (top), 8, 9 (top); Yassie/ Wikipedia, p. 9 (bottom); Jeff Lewis/ Icon SMI/ Corbis, p. 12; Rich Kane/ Icon SMI/ Corbis, p. 13; AiWire/ Newscom, pp. 16-17; AJ Mast/ AP/ Corbis, pp. 18-19; John Angelillo/ UPI/ Newscom, p. 20.